The Fascinating Science of How Animals Use Poop

The Scoop on Poop!

Text and Photographs by Wayne Lynch

To Aubrey, as always

The publisher gratefully acknowledges the support of The Canada Council for the Arts and the Department of Canadian Heritage. We acknowledge the financial support of the Government of Canada through the Book Publishing Industry Development Program for our publishing activities.

National Library of Canada Cataloguing in Publication Data

Lynch, Wayne.
  The scoop on poop

Includes index.
ISBN 1-894004-59-0

1. Feces—Juvenile literature. 2. Animal behavior—Juvenile literature. I. Title.
QP159.L96 2001 j591.5   C2001-910827-3

First published in the United States in 2002

Printed in Canada.
02 03 04 05/ 5 4 3 2

Fifth House Publishers
A Fitzhenry & Whiteside Company
1511 1800 4 Street SW
Calgary, Alberta, Canada
T2S 2S5
www.fitzhenry.ca

In the United States:
Fitzhenry and Whiteside
121 Harvard Avenue, Suite 2
Allston, MA 02134

Scanning by
St. Solo Computer
Graphics Inc.

Contents

Tammar Wallaby: Kangaroo Island, Southern Australia. A young joey watches the world from the safety of its mother's pouch.

1 Poop Is Fascinating Stuff . . . *Really!*

As a boy, I worked on my uncle's dairy farm during the summers. On rainy days, when it was too wet to work in the fields, my uncle would always ask me to clean the barn. That meant shovelling lots of cow patties. I always wondered why cows produced so much poop, and why they always seemed to poop the minute they got into the barn to be milked. When I questioned Uncle Woodford about this, his answer was short and simple. "They poop inside the barn so that there's something for you to do on rainy days." Later, when I grew up and became interested in science and animal behavior, I learned that poop was more than just brown, slippery, smelly muck.

Poop is fascinating stuff! Some wild animals eat it, others use it to send messages, and some squirt it on themselves to cool off. Critters are not the only ones who find animal poop useful. Some people build homes with it, others use it as firewood, and some even toss it around for sport. If you're curious, sit with me and I'll give you the scoop on poop, facts on feces, tips on turds, data on dung, and the goods on guano.

I promise you'll find it interesting, and sometimes funny, and you'll have lots to tell your friends. And when you gross out your parents at dinner, just tell them Dr. Lynch says it's good science.

The author's wife, Aubrey Lang, examines a termite mound in Northern Territory, Australia. Termite mounds are the tallest structures made of poop.

What Is Poop?

Inside an animal's body, food travels through a long tube called the intestine. Animals that eat meat, such as wolves, lions, and humans, have an intestine four to six times longer than their body. Animals that eat mostly plants, like bighorn sheep, have even longer intestines. Theirs may be twenty-five times longer than their body. Seals, for their size, probably have the longest intestine of any wild animal. When scientists measured the intestine of a large elephant seal, it measured twice the length of a football field!

When food arrives in the intestine, chemicals dissolve the food and break it down into fats, proteins, carbohydrates, vitamins, and minerals. Once it's broken down like this, the body can use it. The leftovers mix with bacteria and dead cells from the walls of the intestine. This gut garbage is what we call poop.

The poop of most animals is brown or black. The color comes from old red blood cells, which the body dumps into the intestine to be thrown away.

Poop has
many different names: manure, scats, droppings, whitewash, feces, guano, dung, and stools. It has slang names as well: turd, doo-doo, ca-ca, and a few others we won't mention.

Lion: Masai Mara Game Reserve, Kenya. The heaviest African lion on record was a man-eater that weighed 313 kilograms (690 pounds).

Elephant Seal: Salisbury Plains, South Georgia Island. A bull southern elephant seal bellows from a beach near Antarctica.

The African elephant is the biggest pooper of them all. A ball of elephant poop can weigh one to two kilograms, or two to five pounds (you don't want to get hit on the head with one), and the animal drops more than one hundred of them every day. That's enough poop to fill the trunk of a family car.

The kind of food an animal eats can change the color of its poop. For example, when penguins eat fish, their droppings are white or gray, but when they eat krill— a shrimp-like crustacean—their poop is pink, and when they eat squid, their poop is yellow. Even when an animal stops eating, it still produces poop. Penguins that are fasting produce slimy green doo-doo.

Around most penguin nests, streaks of colored poop radiate out from the edges, like the spokes on a bicycle wheel. Penguins often nest very close together, and a pooping penguin can sometimes hit a neighbor in the face with a blast of gooey guano. The splattered bird never seems too bothered by the accident. It simply shakes its head and lets the whitewash slowly drip off the tip of its beak.

Chinstrap: Deception Island, Antarctic Peninsula. The nest and feathers of this penguin are covered with pink poop, splattered by nearby neighbors.

The blue-footed booby is a tropical sea-bird that nests on the ground. After several weeks, a nest becomes surrounded by a ring of white poop. Adult boobies cannot recognize their own chicks, and only feed chicks that are inside the ring of poop. If a newly hatched booby chick accidentally wanders outside the ring, its parents will not feed it and may even peck it to death if it tries to return.

A streak of poop from an eagle, hawk, or falcon is called a "slice."

Turd Tricks

When a wild bird needs to poop, it usually squirts wherever it happens to be sitting at the time. If you watch an eagle or a hawk perched in a tree or on a telephone pole, it often leans forward and poops just before it flies off. Anything a bird can do to weigh less makes it easier for it to fly.

Alligators, cobras, sharks, killer whales, moose, and many other wild creatures simply poop whenever they feel the urge. They often poop while they are eating. The intestine in these animals empties out at one end to make room for food coming in at the other end.

Some animals poop in special places. For example, wolves, coyotes, red foxes, weasels, and mink often poop in the middle of a trail that they use all the time. Here, their droppings are easy for other animals to see and smell. In Indonesia, a Komodo dragon—the largest lizard in the world—may spend ten minutes flicking its long forked tongue over a fresh dropping it finds along a game trail.

Why do some animals poop in a special place? For one thing, poop is a good way to leave a message. The smell of poop is different in a young animal than in an adult. It's also different between a male and a female. Female animals often use the smell

Below – Caiman: Pantanal wetlands, Brazil.
The common caiman, a close relative of the alligator,
lives in the wetlands of Central and South America.

Above – Komodo Dragon: Komodo Island, Indonesia. The Komodo dragon uses its strong claws to dig burrows and climb, and during courtship.

Indian Rhino: Kaziranga National Park, India. The thick skin of the
Indian one-horned rhinoceros protects it from branches and sharp grass.

of their poop like perfume, to attract a partner. Also, the smell of poop may be unique for each animal, and identify the owner, like a fingerprint or a photograph. Day after day, a rhinoceros poops in the same places. Its piles of dung can get very large. In India, I found a huge pile of rhino dung that covered an area as large as a kitchen floor. When rhinos visit a dung pile, they scrape their feet in the poop until their feet are really smelly. When the rhinos leave, they spread the smell every time they take a step. This tells other rhinos that they are in the neighborhood.

When an animal finds another animal's dropping on the trail, it helps it decide what to do next. If the poop is fresh, it serves as a warning not to continue and announces that the trail ahead is closed. If the poop is not so fresh, the animal may continue, but with caution. And if the dropping is old, then the animal can keep going and not worry about running into a rival. Hikers can also use the freshness of animal poop to learn which wild critters recently used the trail.

Many animals defend a territory. Some of them use their poop to keep trespassers away. The spotted hyena of Africa is a good example of this. The hyena lives in groups called clans. All of the clan members poop along the boundary of their hunting territory. The spotted hyena is one of the few animals that can crush bones with its powerful jaws and then swallow them. When it has been eating bones, its droppings are bright white in color. These white droppings clearly mark the borders of the clan's territory. Once, in the Serengeti Plains of East Africa, I watched a clan

A hibernating bear doesn't poop at all. When it is hibernating in its winter den, it may not poop for six months or more. But when it finally does, the first dropping may be a whopper. One man in Alaska found a grizzly bear dropping that was as long as his arm, and thicker than his wrist.

of hyenas kill a zebra on the boundary between their hunting grounds and their neighbors'. The neighbors raced to the kill, and the two clans fought fiercely over the carcass. When the fight was over, members of both clans—many of them wounded and bleeding—pooped nearby. It was their way of declaring that the boundary was still the same.

Spotted Hyena: Masai Mara Game Reserve, Kenya. Among spotted hyenas, the females are in charge. They are larger, stronger, and more aggressive than male hyenas.

2 Poop Tarts

When food travels through the intestine, some of the nutrition in the food passes out with the poop. That's because the animal's body can't break it down and absorb it all. It's the same when you eat corn on the cob. Later on you can see some of the corn in your feces because your body can't digest all of the kernels. Animal poop often contains this kind of undigested food. That's why some animals eat poop.

Arctic Fox: Hudson Bay, Canada. An arctic fox follows the fresh tracks of a hunting polar bear.

In the far corners of the Arctic, the sea ice is frozen most of the year and food is always hard to find. The polar bear—a large, powerful meat-eater—hunts seals when they come to the surface of the ice to breathe. Two arctic animals, the ivory gull and the arctic fox, commonly follow polar bears on the ice to feed on the scraps of food they leave behind after they kill a seal. But the hungry scavengers eat more than the leftovers. They also gobble up the bear's poop for any undigested food it might contain. In Africa, jackals, spotted hyenas, and hooded vultures eagerly eat the droppings of lions for the same reason. In North America, the turkey vulture also has a taste for turds. This feathered skinhead eats coyote droppings and the fishy feces of sea lions.

One of my favorite birds in Antarctica is the snowy sheathbill. It's an ugly white bird with a pink warty face and terrible table manners. Nothing is too rotten, smelly, or disgusting to spoil a sheathbill's appetite. I watched one pick at the crusty scabs on the neck of a wounded elephant seal. Later, it pulled apart and ate the rotting carcass of a dead seal pup, and it picked at every kind of poop it found on the beach. The most amazing sheathbill story I know involved a chinstrap penguin. A sheathbill was wandering through a colony of nesting chinstraps when one of the penguins leaned over and pooped. In the gooey poop was a long tapeworm that had been living inside the penguin's intestine. Even worse, the head of the tapeworm was still attached inside the chinstrap. When the long white worm slowly began to crawl back inside the penguin's rear end, the hungry sheathbill came to the rescue and grabbed the tapeworm and made a meal out of it. The final score: sheathbill one; tapeworm zero.

Top – Sheathbill: Hercules Bay, South Georgia Island. The scientific name of the pale-faced sheathbill is Chionis alba, *which means snow white, but the sheathbill has neither the looks nor the table manners of the famous princess.*

Bottom – Hooded Vulture: Serengeti National Park, Tanzania. The bare face of the hooded vulture flushes deep red when the bird is hungry or excited.

A phids are tiny insects that use their long, tube-like mouths to suck sap out of plants. Ants often form a partnership with aphids. The ants protect the tiny aphids from predators such as ladybug beetles and wasps. In exchange, the aphids poop a sugary syrup, which the ants love to eat.

In autumn, some ants will even carry the aphids underground to protect them for the winter. Then, in the spring, the ants bring the aphids out again for another season of sap sucking.

Dung Beetles

When it comes to dining on dung, beetles do it best. There are seven thousand kinds of dung beetles. In the Amazon rainforest, fifty different beetles may fight over a pile of monkey turds. The beetles are attracted to the poop by its smell, and the first ones may arrive just two minutes after the poop goes plop.

With so many beetles coming to dinner at the same time, it's not surprising that they use the dung in different ways. Some dung beetles are house-hunters, others are tunnellers, and some are rollers.

The house-hunting beetles are usually pretty small. They burrow inside the juicy poop, where they eat and rest and eat and rest. When they are tired of resting, they eat some more. The tunnelling dung beetles are usually bigger than the house-hunters.

The tunnellers dig a deep burrow in the ground, underneath the dung. At the end of the tunnel they store a pile of poop, sometimes as large as a man's fist. While they are packing in the poop, they lay eggs inside the dung. When they are finished, they fill the tunnel with dirt to hide the dung from other beetles. After the eggs hatch, the baby beetles, called grubs, feed on the juicy, rich dung.

Dung Beetle: Das Emas National Park, S.W. Brazil. This beautiful dung beetle is from the Pantanal grasslands.

The most interesting dung beetles are the rollers. In Africa, you may see hundreds of these beetles swarming over a steaming pad of fresh buffalo dung. The male rollers bite off wads of dung and roll it into a ball

Even Poop can become fossilized and turn to stone. Fossil poop is called "coprolite." Some coprolites are older than the dinosaurs.

Dung Beetle: Floral City, Central Florida, United States.
A beetle rolls away a fresh ball of deer poop.

using their rear legs. Once the ball is big enough, which is usually larger than the beetle itself, the male finds a partner. Then the couple leaves on a honeymoon. The male rolls the poop and the female follows behind or sometimes rides on the top of the poop ball. When the beetles find a good spot, they dig a hole and bury themselves and the poop underground and feast on the feces for several days. The female, after stuffing herself with delicious poop, lays an egg inside the leftovers, and the honeymoon is over. The egg hatches after a couple of weeks, and the white, wiggly grub feeds on the poop until it grows into an adult beetle.

Koalas live in Australia. They eat the leaves of eucalyptus trees, which are hard to digest. The mother koala has bacteria in her intestine that helps her break down the tough leaves. A baby koala needs these bacteria so that it can switch from a diet of milk to a diet of eucalyptus leaves. But where does it get them? If you guessed that it eats its mother's poop, you're right. The mother's poop is full of helpful bacteria that the baby needs.

Koala: Queensland, Australia. A baby koala rides inside its mother's pouch until it is six months old. After that it rides on her back.

Recycled Poop

Many animals such as moose, muskoxen, zebras, and camels eat grass, leaves, bark, twigs, and buds. Most of these plant foods are very hard to digest, so these animals have little helpers living in their intestine. The helpers are special bacteria and other tiny organisms that break down the tough plants that the animals eat. Rabbits and hares also eat plants that are hard to digest. But they have another way to get the most from their diet. They eat their own poop.

Many of you will have seen the dry, round droppings that rabbits leave on the ground when they have been feeding in your family's garden or flower bushes. Rabbits also produce a second kind of poop that is soft, moist, and covered with slime.

Arctic Hare: Ellesmere Island National Park Reserve, Canada. Like all hares, this mammal from the Canadian High Arctic eats its own poop.

Termites are small blind insects that are the size of ants. Millions of termites may live in a single colony, and together they sometimes build castles as tall as a house. The insects use their own poop to cement their houses together.

Termite mound: Northern Territory, Australia. The shape of this termite mound protects the colony from overheating in the hot tropical sun.

Termites: Das Emas National Park, Brazil. These termites work quickly to repair their colony after it was raided by an anteater.

These droppings never hit the ground.

The rabbit puts its head between its legs and eats the droppings as soon as they come out its rear. It swallows the soft poop whole, without chewing it. The poop travels through the animal's intestine a second time. By recycling its poop the rabbit gets as much goodness as it can out of its food. The second time around the rabbit poops the dry round pellets I talked about earlier.

A Poop Quiz

Match the poop with the pooper. — Look on page 32 for the answers.

A – Arctic Fox

B – Spotted Hyena

C – Spruce Grouse

D – Moose

E – Giant Tortoise

F – Black Bear

1 – A scat with curly ends

2 – Pile of poop with undigested berries

3 – White lumps of powdered bone

4 – A grassy wad

5 – Compact plug of conifer needles

6 – Dry brown pellets

3 The Power of Poop

Frilled Lizard: Kakadu National Park, Australia. The flap of loose skin surrounding the head of this lizard makes the animal look larger and more fearsome than it really is.

In Nature, poop helps wild plants grow better. For example, many trees in the tropical rainforest are hollow inside. Animals, especially bats and anteaters, like to hide inside hollow trees. When they poop, their droppings fall to the ground, which makes the soil richer and helps the trees to grow. It's a similar story in the dry forests of Australia. There, many of the trees, called eucalyptus or gum trees, have very soft wood in the center of their trunks. Termites eat the soft wood and hollow out the trees. Afterwards, many Australian animals including possums, sugar gliders, parrots, owls, pythons, frilled lizards, and frogs move inside. It's a perfect place for the animals to hide from their enemies and stay warm and dry when it is rainy and windy outside. The tree provides the animals with a good home and in return it gets a reward—all the poop the animals drop inside helps the tree grow larger and stronger.

Another proof of the power in poop involves bears and berries. When a black bear eats a mouthful of berries, it usually swallows the fruit without much chewing. This means that the seeds inside the berries don't get crushed. They usually pass safely through the bear's intestine and come out in its poop. What is surprising is that the seeds that are eaten by a black bear grow better than if you took the seeds directly from

Lichens are some of the toughest plants in the world. There is no place too cold, too windy, or too dry for them to grow. One tough lichen, the orange jewel lichen, grows best where there is bird poop. Eagles, hawks, and falcons often perch on the same rocks, day after day, to hunt and watch for trespassers. While they are waiting they often poop on the rocks. The poop makes jewel lichens grow especially well, and the rocks soon become covered with these bright orange plants. Scientists who study birds of prey fly in airplanes and look for these colorful rocks, which are easy to see from the air. This helps them find the birds.

Above – Lichen: Vuntut National Park, Canada. This pile of lichen-covered rocks at the top of a hill in Yukon was used by snowy owls, eagles, and hawks as a hunting perch.

Left – Golden Eagle: Alberta, Canada. The golden eagle has a wingspan taller than an adult man.

the berries and planted them yourself. Biologists think that the chemicals inside a bear's intestine make it easier for the seeds to soak up water and oxygen. Once the seeds drop to the ground inside a bear's poop, they have a better chance of growing into another berry bush. So, when a bear eats berries, it sometimes plants new berry bushes with its poop.

Getting Cool with Poop

In summer, when you are hot, your body sweats. Sweat is mostly water. When the sweat on your skin evaporates, or dries, it cools you off. Hikers lost in the hot desert sometimes don't have enough water in their body to sweat, so they can't stay cool. To survive, they can rub their own urine on their arms and legs. It works just like sweat, and helps them cool off. The poop of many animals and birds contains lots of water, and they can get cool with their own poop. Some birds squirt liquid poop on their legs when they get too hot. Storks and many vultures chill out this way. They can squirt themselves every two minutes if they need to. A stork that is overheated will squirt one leg at a time, and go from side to side, until it finally cools down.

Marabou Stork: Masai Mara Game Reserve, Kenya. The marabou stork normally has gray legs, but this one has squirted itself with white liquid poop.

Motherly Love

For the first month of its life, a white-tailed deer fawn will not poop unless its mother licks its bottom. Normally, a fawn spends the day hiding in tall grass or beneath bushes, while its mother is away feeding. The mother comes back three or fours times during the day to nurse the fawn. While it is nursing, the mother nuzzles the fawn's bottom. This tells the young animal that it's time to poop and pee. The mother drinks the pee and eats the droppings. By doing this she gets rid of strong smells that might attract a hungry predator, such as a coyote, wolf, or bear. I found out that other animals are like this when I cared for an

Gray Kangaroo: Wilson's Promontory National Park, Australia. A young kangaroo will poop inside its mother's pouch until it is one year old.

White-tailed Deer: Southern Saskatchewan, Canada. While a pair of fawns nurses, their mother eats their poop and drinks their urine.

24

orphan black bear cub. The cub would not poop unless I wiped its bottom with a warm, wet paper towel. Thank goodness that worked because I was not prepared to use my tongue like its mother would.

The Arctic Tern

nests on the ground. If a hungry fox or wolf comes near the nest, the tern swoops over the predators, pecking them and spraying them with smelly poop.

The mothers of young deer, moose, elk, and gazelles usually stop eating their baby's poop once the baby is about a month old. That's when it is big enough to run well and escape from predators. The mother gray kangaroo is not so lucky. The kangaroo is a special kind of mammal, called a marsupial. Marsupials raise their babies in a pouch on the mother's stomach. A baby kangaroo, called a joey, sometimes lives in its mother's pouch until it is almost a year old. During that time, the mother licks the joey's bottom and eats its poop. That's the only way she can keep her pouch clean. Now that's motherly love.

Poop for Protection

Did you ever wonder why poop smells so bad? The stinkers are the bacteria that normally live in the intestine and help an animal digest its food, and that's a good thing. But these bacteria also produce smelly chemicals, which give poop its bad smell. The poop of carnivores, such as weasels, civets, and otters, smells the worst, although humans can sometimes outstink them all. Many snakes also have smelly poop and use it to protect themselves. When you pick up a garter snake, it coils around your hand,

Cottonmouth: Everglades National Park, United States. When it is threatened, this venomous snake uses the white lining of its mouth as a warning.

25

and you immediately notice that it stinks. These harmless snakes squirt smelly poop over themselves when a predator grabs them. Sometimes, if they are lucky, the strong smell convinces the predator to let them go.

Many snakes use poop as a weapon, even when they have other ways to defend themselves. The giant anaconda of South America is the largest snake in the world. It sometimes weighs more than a big man. This monster snake has a mouth full of sharp teeth, but when it feels frightened, it squirts bad-smelling poop. Another snake that really stinks is the venomous cottonmouth of the southern United States.

Yellow Anaconda: Pantanal, Brazil. Like its giant relative, the yellow anaconda also squirts smelly poop to discourage predators.

The cottonmouth has long curved fangs, and it can inject deadly venom into its enemies, but it also uses poop to scare away a predator. I once helped a scientist catch a cottonmouth in a swamp in Florida. When we grabbed the snake with special tongs, it thrashed its tail back and forth wildly, splashing both of us with rotten-smelling, fishy poop. Yuck.

Looking Like a Turd

Insects have a tough life. Everything wants to eat them. To fool predators, many of them pretend to look like bird droppings. These tricky insects are colored brown, black, and white, and twist their bodies to disguise their shape. Then they sit in the middle of a leaf and look icky just like a bird dropping. To make their disguise even better, some beetles in South America grow special swellings on their legs that look like seeds stuck in a wet blob of bird poop.

Certain crab spiders also pretend to look like poop to hide themselves from their next meal. Since butterflies often land on poop to sip up water and salt, the spider's disguise usually helps it attract a tasty meal. Many types of flies also lay their eggs in fresh dung, and the spider tries to fool them as well. One group of spiders even produces a chemical that smells like poop. This helps them attract even more insects.

4 People and Poop

Farmers all over the world spread poop on their fields. They call it manure, and it makes their crops grow better. In China, the farmers carry heavy baskets of pig and cow manure on their shoulders and throw it on the fields with their bare hands. In North America, the farmers keep their hands clean. They use special machines called manure spreaders to toss the turds around. These machines shred the manure and throw it out the back while the farmer tows the machine around the fields with a tractor. I did this job when I was a boy, working on my uncle's farm, and I soon found out why he let me do it. Sometimes the manure spreader would toss a lump of poop forward instead of backwards, and I would get whacked on the back of the head with a big lump of poop.

Peruvian Boobies: Isla Choros, Northern Chile. A large colony of nesting Peruvian boobies may produce tons of guano every year.

Cow manure is food for crops and helps the crops grow, but guano works even better. The name guano (pronounced GWAH-no) comes from a Native word in Peru that means seabird poop. Along the coast of Peru, there are more than twenty small islands where millions of cormorants, boobies, and pelicans nest. The birds nested, and pooped, on these islands long before people came to South America. At one time, the guano on some of the islands was deep enough to bury a fifteen-storey building.

Guano is one of the best natural fertilizers, and farmers have used it for thousands of years. One hundred and fifty years ago in Peru, there was a guano rush, just like a gold rush. Many ships from Europe and the United States sailed to Peru to gather the precious seabird poop. In 1860, for example, over four hundred ships loaded up with guano. In those years, guano was the most important product that Peru had to sell, and the money that Peru made from selling it was enough to run the entire country. Today, people still collect small amounts of guano on the islands.

More Facts on Feces

People use poop for more things than fertilizer. In the mountains of China, the peasants collect the droppings of certain moth caterpillars and use this poop to brew a fragrant black tea called "chongha." They think the tea helps their digestion. In South America, people collect the droppings of a caterpillar that feeds on the coca plant. Why? Because, in this case, the insect poop contains the drug cocaine.

If you look closely at a ball of elephant dung, a pile of moose pellets, or a dried cow pie, you will see pieces of plants, and sometimes bits of wood. The early pioneers, who settled on the prairies of North America,

In Egypt, bats often live inside the ancient pyramids, and their droppings sometimes carry disease. The scientific name of the disease is histoplasmosis, but it is commonly called "the curse of the mummy's tomb."

Cow patties: Guwahati, Assam, India. Near a farmer's house, a collection of cow patties dries in the sun. They will be burned later.

gathered wagonloads of dry "buffalo chips" to burn in their stoves instead of wood. Buffalo chips were free, they burned slowly and hot, and they smelled like grass. To the pioneers, dried dung was very valuable. Today, in places where trees and wood are scarce, the local people still use dried animal dung as fuel for their cooking fires. In India, rural people collect cow manure and bring it into the cities where they sell it by the bundle, like firewood. A bundle of five cow chips costs about ten cents. In the Andes Mountains of South America, the Quecha Natives use the dried dung of guanacos and vicunas to light their fires, and in the Sahara Desert, the Tuareg people use camel dung.

The wood fibers in animal dung gave some people a different idea. In Canada, an art teacher, named Cyndi Foster, uses horse droppings and elk pellets to make paper. Check it out at www.expertcanmore.net/earthpaper. Foster says that every poop has its own smell. Horse poop smells like oatmeal, and elk poop smells like grass clippings. Luckily, her poop paper doesn't phew. In Africa, other artists use dried elephant dung and rhino dung to make their own brand of "designer" paper.

TOSSING TURDS Believe it or not, tossing turds is a popular game, at least in some parts of the United States. The town of Beaver, Oklahoma, calls itself the "Cow Chip Throwing Capital of the World." Every April, the town celebrates the World Championship Cow Chip Throw. The cow chips are collected in early spring, and each tosser gets to choose his or her own chip from a wagonload of them. Some contestants spin around and fling their chip like an Olympic discus thrower, while others toss it like a Frisbee. Most chip chuckers, however, fling their chips overhand, as they would a baseball. The record distance for a flying chip is 47 metres, or 155 feet, about half the length of a football field.

Photograph © Joc Van Os

Namanga, Kenya. A Masai woman smears fresh cow manure on the outside of a new house she is building.

If you've ever accidentally stepped in a fresh cow pie, you know how sticky poop can be. Because of this, people in some parts of the world use poop to plaster their houses. The Masai people in East Africa build huts of sticks and grass, which are shaped like a loaf of bread. To make their homes waterproof, the people cover the outside with a thick layer of cattle dung. In the Masai culture, women are the house builders. They mix fresh cattle dung and water with their hands, then spread the muck over their houses. The dung dries quickly in the hot sun, and it keeps the inside of the house dry for many months afterwards. Every so often, they repair the house by adding more dung to fill in the cracks.

Dung Detectives

Scientists often examine the dung of an animal they are studying to see what the animal is eating. With practice, it's easy for them to recognize the ear bones of a fish, the beak of a squid, the claws of a lemming, the tooth of a shrew, or the seeds of a raspberry. Using a microscope, a good dung detective can even recognize whether a hair belongs to a moose, a mouse, or a monkey. This is possible because the surface of every hair is covered with tiny scales that look different in almost every mammal.

Graduate researcher Anne Holcroft examines a black bear dropping.

Since poop is made up of leftovers from a meal anything that is completely digested in the intestine will not show up in a dropping. This is the biggest problem when poop is used to find out what an animal eats. For example, a dung detective may never know that a bear ate a mouthful of mushrooms, or a large lump of meat, because both of these foods are completely digested and leave no clues in the animal's poop.

Wild animal

droppings can sometimes be dangerous to humans. The poop may contain parasites and other diseases, and should never be touched. Scientists use plastic gloves to protect themselves. Biologists who study bats inside caves even wear special masks so they don't inhale dangerous germs.

Whenever I walk in the woods I always hope to see wildlife, but often I don't. Sometimes, all I see are tracks. When I am lucky, I find some poop. When this happens, I try to figure out which animal it was and what it was doing. Why did it poop in that particular spot? I try to imagine what was happening in the animal's life at that moment in time. This habit of mine makes every hike in the outdoors an exciting experience, and I come home happy. In this book I've told you many of the fascinating facts I have learned about the science of poop. So, the next time you wander in the woods, keep an eye on the ground. There are secrets to discover in a pile of poop.

Index

Ostrich: Serengeti National Park, Tanzania. Ostriches are the world's largest living birds.

Answers to quiz on page 20

A – 1
B – 3
C – 5
D – 6
E – 4
F – 2